Gretchen Bitte
Dennis Johns
Donna Pri
Sylvia Ramir
K. Lynn Savage, Series Editor

Ventures
Multilevel Lesson Planner

CAMBRIDGE
UNIVERSITY PRESS

CAMBRIDGE UNIVERSITY PRESS
Cambridge, New York, Melbourne, Madrid, Cape Town, Singapore, São Paulo, Delhi, Dubai, Tokyo

Cambridge University Press
32 Avenue of the Americas, New York, NY 10013-2473, USA

www.cambridge.org
Information on this title: www.cambridge.org/9780521739733

First published 2009
2nd printing 2010
Printed in the United States of America

A catalog record for this book is available from the British Library

ISBN 978-0-521-73973-3 Multilevel Lesson Planner

Cambridge University Press has no responsibility for the persistence or
accuracy of URLs for external or third-party Internet Web sites referred to in
this publication, and does not guarantee that any content on such Web sites is,
or will remain, accurate or appropriate. Information regarding prices, travel
timetables, and other factual information given in this work are correct at
the time of first printing, but Cambridge University Press does not guarantee
the accuracy of such information thereafter.

Book design and layout services: Adventure House, NYC

....

Contents

Introduction

Meeting the needs of students in any classroom is always a challenge. Meeting the needs of students in the multilevel classroom is an even bigger challenge. It requires ongoing assessment of the students' very different needs and expectations; it requires diligent and potentially time-consuming lesson preparation; it requires careful selection of appropriate grouping strategies and classroom management; and not least of all, it requires judicious selection of materials to exploit the learning possibilities unique to the multilevel classroom.

Ventures Multilevel Lesson Planner has been written to simplify the preparation for and address the challenges of the multilevel teaching situation.

The chapters:
- describe the multilevel classroom
- define what teachers need to know in order to promote success and create a learning community
- present the key features in the *Ventures* series that make it the appropriate resource for the multilevel setting
- introduce the Multilevel Organizers to streamline class preparation time
- promote pedagogically sound instructional strategies and materials that require limited teacher preparation

The *Ventures Multilevel Lesson Planner* also includes:
- reproducible Multilevel Organizers: At-A-Glance for each lesson type in the *Ventures* Student's Books
- reproducible Multilevel Organizers: Teaching Steps for each lesson type in the *Ventures* Student's Books
- reproducible Multilevel Lesson Plan Templates to customize lesson planning

The CD-ROM at the back of the *Ventures Multilevel Lesson Planner* includes:
- 21 illustrations selected from the unit-opening pictures in the Student's Books across the series. These visuals support the teaching suggestions in the Organizers that help build community in the classroom, preview

common themes across levels of *Ventures*, and encourage whole-group activities.
- reproducible Multilevel Organizers for each lesson type in the *Ventures* Student's Books
- reproducible Multilevel Lesson Plan Templates for teachers to customize their lesson plans
- reproducible class audio scripts for self-study and self-correction during students' break-out study time

Ventures Multilevel Lesson Planner helps teachers using multiple levels of *Ventures* within a single classroom address the widely divergent needs of students at different levels in the class. Using *Ventures* at levels appropriate for students, the class can become a place in which all students are challenged and all goals are met.

Authors' Acknowledgments

The authors would like to thank the teachers and students in the many multilevel classes we observed, our colleagues who have so generously shared at professional conferences their own experience in teaching adult ESL multilevel classes, and, of course, the students in our own multilevel classes.

The authors would also like to extend their particular thanks to the following reviewers and consultants for their valuable insights and suggestions:

Monica Galvan, San Diego Community College Continuing Education, San Diego, California; **Marilynn Garvey**, Washington Township Community & Continuing Education, Indianapolis, Indiana; **Sara Zarick Gutting**, Adult Education Specialist, Indianapolis, Indiana; **Lois Miller**, Tucson, Arizona; **Barbara Pongsrikul**, Ed.D., San Diego Community College Continuing Education, San Diego, California; **Iryna Scharer-Filatova**, San Diego Community College Continuing Education, San Diego, California; **Linda Selover**; **Laurel Owensby Slater**, San Diego Community College Continuing Education, San Diego, California

Chapter 1

Defining the Multilevel Classroom

What is "the multilevel class"?

This chapter describes two types of multilevel classes:
• level-specific
• non level-specific

It also discusses the following topics:
• grouping strategies
• materials selection

All classes are multilevel in some sense. No two students will ever be exactly the same. Students vary in several ways, including demographic factors such as culture and ethnicity; personal factors such as differences in learning styles, age, and willingness to take risks; and experiential factors such as background knowledge and previous education. Because of these differences, it is often a challenge to provide useful learning activities for all students in the class.

When addressing the needs of students in the multilevel classroom, teachers and administrators need to consider three issues: (1) types of multilevel classes, (2) grouping strategies, and (3) materials. Responses to these issues must support the needs of the teachers and students in their specific multilevel setting in order to help both teachers and students become successful.

Two types of multilevel classes

Level-specific classes

One common multilevel situation occurs in classes that are intended as level-specific classes. Students are generally placed in these classes using a placement test to determine level, but the placement test can result in students of differing abilities in the same class. For example, if a program uses only an oral placement interview, there may be differences among students in their literacy skills. If a program uses only a reading placement test, there may be differences among students in their aural / oral skills.

Even when all four skills are tested for placement purposes, there may be differences among the students. Some students may have barely tested into the level, whereas others may be close to testing out of the level. Moreover, a single student can be at different proficiency levels in different skill areas. For example, a student may be more skilled in listening and speaking than in reading and writing, or more skilled in reading and writing than in listening and speaking. Similarly, a student may have better receptive skills (listening and reading) than productive skills (speaking and writing). Even in the unlikely scenario that all students enter the class at the same level of proficiency in each of the various language skills, students will not all remain at the same level, as different students progress at different rates.

It is this mix of abilities, even within classes created for specific levels, that causes ESL teachers to say, "Every ESL class is a multilevel class."

Non level-specific classes

Non level-specific classes are often referred to in ESL as "one-room classrooms." In these classes, there may be a mix of students ranging from students with no first language literacy skills to students functioning at the highest ESL level. Students in classes like these often have multiple goals and multiple needs.

There are many reasons for offering non level-specific classes. Sometimes a business or elementary school provides on-site classes for their workers or parents. As there may be limited space and times to offer the classes, one or two classes are provided for all the students. Sometimes there are off-site locations close to neighborhoods where students live or work. These locations may include churches, schools, housing projects, and community centers. It is often not feasible to offer more than one or two classes at these locations.

Teachers in these classes often do not have adequate resources available to them. An additional challenge is that these classes are often taught by new instructors. To address the complexity of the multilevel class, it is especially important for the teacher to implement good class-management techniques. Effective class management depends on appropriate classroom grouping strategies and appropriate materials selection.

Grouping strategies

Teachers use a variety of grouping strategies in multilevel classes, including whole group, like-ability groups, cross-ability groups, and individual study.

Whole group

In this grouping strategy, teachers and students work together as a whole class. This strategy is most common in opening and closing a lesson. In the class opening, teachers use whole-group activities to introduce materials and topics. Whole-group activities build community among students in the class and give them the confidence to work in small groups or independently, knowing that they will also have access to the teacher. In the class closing, teachers use whole-group activities to check attainment of skills practiced and to review key points.

Like-ability groups

In like-ability groups, students who have similar proficiency levels are grouped together. Like-ability group activities focus on the development of language skills – such as listening, speaking, reading, and writing – targeted at the specific proficiency level of students in the group. In multilevel classes, the teacher may create several levels of like-ability groups and use these groups to have students work on material specific to their proficiency level.

Cross-ability groups

Cross-ability groups are small groups of three to six students of differing proficiency levels working together on the same task. The ideal cross-ability group has one or two students from each differing proficiency level. Cross-ability groups encourage students to help each other while assuming responsibility for their own learning. An important outcome of this kind of group is the promotion of peer tutoring and community building, which facilitates the whole-group opening and closing portions of the class. Activities that require collaboration – such as projects and cooperative-learning tasks – are especially effective in cross-ability groups.

Individual study

Another important way to promote level-appropriate practice is to have students work independently with level-appropriate materials. Individual student practice gives students the opportunity to direct their own learning. Some appropriate individual materials include handouts or workbooks with answer keys, audio programs and audio scripts for independent listening practice, and reading selections with comprehension activities at or below the students' reading skill levels. When having students work individually, the teacher needs to ensure that students understand how to access the answers and self-correct mistakes.

Materials selection

Teachers in multilevel classes may use the *same*-level materials with all students but have different expectations for different learners, or they may use *different*-level materials that correspond to the different levels of learners in the class.

Same materials

Teachers may choose, or be required to use, the same-level materials for all students. When this occurs, the teacher will have different expectations for

different students. This is often the approach taken in a level-specific class. The following describe examples of using the same materials with different expectations.

Visual materials The same visual can be used to elicit different levels of language. For example, for vocabulary practice, low-level students in a multilevel class can point to and name objects and actions; mid-level students can spell aloud the words that low-level students identify; high-level students can write the words on the board or make sentences using the words.

Teachers can also use visuals to ask level-appropriate questions when introducing a theme or topic. Low-level students can answer *Yes / No* questions (*Is the man happy?*); mid-level students can provide short answers (*What is the man wearing?*); and high-level students can answer broader questions (*Tell me about the picture.*).

Reading material Students, regardless of reading proficiency, can work on the same text as long as the tasks are level-appropriate. For example, for vocabulary practice, low-level students can find a word in the text; mid-level students can look up the definition in a dictionary; and high-level students can create original sentences using the targeted vocabulary.

Listening material Playing or reading the same recorded material to all students regardless of level also works successfully in a multilevel classroom. After listening, low-level students can answer very general questions about the content (*Who is talking? What are they talking about?*); mid-level students can answer questions about detail (*What do you hear? What is happening?*); and high-level students can paraphrase and summarize.

Different materials

Another approach to selection of materials in multilevel classes is to use different-level materials. That is, the teacher chooses, or develops, different materials that match the different levels of students in the class. This is often the case in the non level-specific classroom. Three strategies for using different materials are through textbooks, self-access materials, and learning stations.

Textbooks Some textbook series use the same themes in the same sequence across the various levels in the series. For example, if Unit 3 is about health in Book 1, Unit 3 in Book 2 is also about health. Some teachers who discover such a series have different students use different levels of the student's books or workbooks within the series. That is, after determining the proficiency level of students, the teacher assigns a specific-level textbook within the series based on each student's proficiency level.

Self-access materials Self-access materials enable students to work without a teacher, allowing the teacher to focus on other groups in the class.

Self-access materials have clear directions so that students can do the activities with minimal assistance from the teacher. These materials may also have answer keys so that students can correct their own work. Workbooks are a common example of self-access materials. Teachers can find self-access materials online, and many books have accompanying computer programs that are especially helpful in promoting individual practice, review, and reinforcement of learning.

Learning stations Learning stations are places where students can perform an activity, check their answers, and then move on to the next activity at another learning station. Teachers set up stations in different locations in a classroom or an adjoining room. At these stations, students work on materials that focus on different skill areas. There may be stations for listening, for grammar, for vocabulary, and so forth. Students may choose a station or teachers may direct how students proceed through them. An important requirement is

that the teachers provide clear direction and tasks for students to perform as well as ways for students to check performance. There are generally answer keys at each station so students can be accountable for their own learning. Teachers may devote a specific amount of time during each class for students to work at these learning stations.

SUMMARY

Multilevel classes are usually described in two ways: *level-specific* and *non level-specific*. Teachers use a variety of grouping strategies in multilevel classes, including *whole group*, *like-ability group*, *cross-ability group*, and *individual study*. Two approaches to materials selection often used for multilevel classes are using the same materials with different expectations and using different materials with leveled expectations.

Chapter 2 describes how the *Ventures* series addresses the multilevel classroom, facilitates grouping strategies, and simplifies the selection and creation of materials for both level-specific and non level-specific classes.

Ventures *in the Multilevel Classroom*

How does *Ventures* address the "multi" in every ESL classroom?

This chapter discusses the following topics:
• *Ventures* in the level-specific class
• *Ventures* in the non level-specific class

It also discusses the following topics:
• *Ventures* placement strategies
• monitoring progress

Let's take a look at two multilevel situations:

Situation 1. "Every ESL class is a multilevel class."

In a community college classroom, 20 students have taken a written placement test and have tested into a low-intermediate level class. Some of the students have been surrounded by an English-speaking environment for several years and can speak at an intermediate level. Other students have only just come to an English-speaking environment and are very hesitant speakers.

Because of this difference, the teacher recognizes that he has students at different levels in listening and speaking, even though they have been grouped together in the same low-intermediate class. He knows he should group students according to their abilities and interests.

Situation 2. "One-room classrooms"

A teacher offers a multilevel class at a community center. The classroom has one board, three large tables, folding chairs, and 20 students. A 24-year-old student with a college degree is sitting next to a 60-year-old student who never attended school in her native country. The 24-year-old student wants to find a job and is eager to improve his English for very practical reasons. The 60-year-old student is a refugee who left her country due to cultural problems and war. She is trying to adapt to this life change.

The teacher knows that she should assess students' needs, plan meaningful activities that are level appropriate for each student, and group students according to interests and abilities.

This chapter focuses on how the *Ventures* series addresses the multilevel situation in both of these types of classes.

Ventures in the level-specific class

Often in level-specific classes, in which only one level of a Student's Book is used, the level of students' skills and the amount of practice they need to master language skills and competencies vary greatly. There may be students who need either more or less challenging activities than those in the Student's Book, or who would like additional practice at the level of the Student's Book. For these classrooms, the *Ventures* series provides a book of photocopiable worksheets called *Add Ventures*. These multilevel worksheets provide three different levels of activity for each lesson in the Student's Book. These three levels target three different types of students:

☑■■ Students who need additional practice that is at a level below that of the Student's Book

■☑■ Students who need additional practice at the same level as the Student's Book

■■☑ Students who need additional practice that is at a level above that of the Student's Book

Add Ventures offers three worksheets for each lesson in a unit, one for each type of student. This not only enables the teacher to address variation among students, but it also enables the teacher to move a student among the three levels, depending on the student's proficiency within the skill area. For example, a student who is more proficient in aural / oral skills than in reading and writing skills may do the "above level" worksheets in listening (Lesson A) and speaking (Lessons B and C) and the "below level" worksheets in reading (Lesson D) and writing (Lesson E). Similarly, a student who is more proficient in reading and writing skills than in aural / oral skills may do the "below level" worksheets in listening (Lesson A) and speaking (Lessons B and C) and the "above level" worksheets in reading (Lesson D) and writing (Lesson E).

Teachers can use *Add Ventures* in a variety of ways. Some teachers assign a worksheet to students; some teachers let students choose which worksheet they want to complete; and some students work through all three worksheets. The worksheets can be used in class or outside of class for reinforcement.

In class, *Add Ventures* can be used with the like-ability and cross-ability grouping strategies described in Chapter 1. In like-ability groups, students at the same level of skill can work together on the same tasks. For example, students who need the most support can work together on the "below level" worksheets while those who need the least support can work together on the "above level" worksheets. In cross-ability groups, students at different skill levels can work together on their own level-specific worksheets. In these cases, the mixed ability of such groups encourages peer teaching and peer correction as well as community building.

The same or similar content across the three worksheets in a lesson means that teachers can bring students together as a whole class to review the answers; although the tasks vary in difficulty, the answers across the three worksheets are the same.

There is an *Add Ventures* to support Student's Books 1, 2, 3, and 4.

To accompany the *Ventures* Basic level, there are also three tiers of activities. However, at the basic level, the multilevel aspect of classes is most often based on the literacy level of students; therefore, this three-tiered approach is not addressed through *Add Ventures* but rather through two different workbooks, the *Ventures* Basic Workbook and the *Ventures* Basic Literacy Workbook. The assignment of one or the other of the workbooks would depend on the literacy level of the individual student as follows.

1. For students who are pre-, non-, or semiliterate in their own language, the first page for each lesson in the Basic Literacy Workbook provides both an introduction to and practice of letter recognition and stroke order.

2. For students who are literate in their first language and can transfer the concepts of literacy from that language to English, the second page for each lesson in the Basic Literacy Workbook provides practice with recognizing and writing the words and phrases that appear in the Basic Student's Book.

3. For students who are literate in their own language and have some familiarity with the Roman alphabet, the Basic Workbook provides written practice to reinforce the lessons in the Basic Student's Book. It assumes that students can already make a connection between spoken and written English.

Ventures in the non level-specific class

While *Add Ventures* can be used in level-specific classes, one way to address the needs of students in non level-specific classes is to use more than one level of the textbooks in a single series. *Ventures* was written with these classes in mind. As a multilevel textbook series, it incorporates four commonalities across the different levels of the Student's Books and Workbooks.

Common themes

The themes for the same units are the same across levels of *Ventures*. For example, the theme for Unit 1 in all five Student's Books is *Personal information*. The theme for Unit 2 in all five Student's Books is *At school*. For Unit 3, the theme is *Friends and family*, and so on. Because of these common themes across levels, activities to open and close the class can focus on the common theme and engage the whole class regardless of the level of Student's Book a student is using.

Same lesson sequencing within the unit

The sequencing of the lessons within units is the same across levels. Consequently, students across proficiency levels work on the same language skill in the same lesson. For example, regardless of which level of Student's Book they use, all students working on Lesson C are working on grammar; all students working on Lesson D are working on reading; all students working on Lesson E are working on writing, and so on. Because of this sequencing, the class closing can focus on assessing learning in the same language skill area across the different proficiency skills.

Same-activity sequencing within the lesson

The sequencing of activities within lessons is the same across levels. That is, whether the student is using the Basic Student's Book or Student's Book 4, the sequencing of activities is the same. Here is a summary:

- Lesson A activities follow the sequence of **1 Talk about the picture** and **2 Listening**.
- Lesson B and C activities follow the sequence of **1 Focus**, **2 Practice**, and **3 Communicate**.
- Lesson D activities follow the sequence of **1 Before you read**, **2 Read**, and **3 After you read**.
- Lesson E activities follow the sequence of **1 Before you write**, **2 Write**, and **3 After you write**.
- Lesson F activities follow the sequence of **1 Life-skills reading**, **2 Fun with language**, and **3 Wrap up**.

This predictability allows students to work at the same time on the same lesson and sections of the lesson but in their own level-specific books. It helps students to function independently of the teacher and gives teachers more ease in assigning and managing students in like-ability and cross-ability groups.

Tools for independent study

For each level in the *Ventures* series there are two tools that facilitate independent work and self-access.

- The self-study CD that comes at the back of each Student's Book provides models of language. Exercises in the Student's Book and on the self-study CD are indicated by an icon SELF-STUDY AUDIO CD in the Student's Book. Students can listen to the CD on their own or within a group when the teacher is not working with the group.
- Each level of *Ventures* has an accompanying Workbook with answer key which makes it possible for students to correct their own work. This encourages students within a group to work independently or in pairs, freeing the teacher to work with other groups.

Taken together, the four commonalities across the levels of the *Ventures* series – common themes, the same lesson sequencing within units, the same activity sequencing within lessons, and the two tools for independent study – simplify the use of multiple books in a classroom. They support a sense of community within the class since students at different levels are all working on the same theme and language skill area. Most importantly, they save valuable teacher time by reducing the need for materials development.

Placement strategies

How can testing determine the appropriate level of Ventures Student's Book?

Each level in the *Ventures* series correlates to the different instructional levels described in the National Reporting System (NRS).

National Reporting System levels	Ventures Student's Books
Beginning Literacy	*Basic*
Beginning Low	*Ventures 1*
Beginning High	*Ventures 2*
Intermediate Low	*Ventures 3*
Intermediate High	*Ventures 4*

For more information on the National Reporting System, see their Web site (www.nrsweb.org).

Ventures is also correlated to national standardized assessments, such as CASAS, the Comprehensive

Adult Student Assessment System (www.CASAS.org), and BEST, Basic English Skills Test (www.cal.org/best). Teachers can determine which level of Student's Book to assign students based on their scores on these standardized assessments.

Another way to place students is by using the *Ventures* Placement Test (see www.cambridge.org/venturesplacement). This placement test is a 40-item, multiple-choice, paper-and-pencil test that focuses on reading and grammar recognition. The questions are based on the objectives, content, and language of the five levels of the *Ventures* series. How students score on the placement test determines which *Ventures* level is most appropriate.

Of course, measures for placement also need to take into consideration the students' attitudes about language learning and their level of confidence. The less secure students will do better when placed in a level slightly below where they test; the more confident students may do better when placed in a level above where they test.

How can testing determine the number of like-ability groups?

In the non level-specific class, the number of students scoring at the various levels will determine the number of groups, the number of students in each group, and the levels of *Ventures* Student's Book.

Let's take, as an example, a group of 12 students and their test scores on the 40-item *Ventures* Placement Test.

Student	Test score (# correct)
Student #1	12
Student #2	2
Student #3	14
Student #4	25
Student #5	5
Student #6	3
Student #7	18
Student #8	11
Student #9	8
Student #10	10
Student #11	21
Student #12	16

Using a chart that correlates test scores with a level of Student's Book, each student's level can be identified.

Test score (# correct)	Student's Book level
0 (few or no literacy skills)	*Ventures Basic & Ventures Literacy Workbook*
1–4	*Ventures Basic*
5–13	*Ventures 1*
14–22	*Ventures 2*
23–31	*Ventures 3*
32–40	*Ventures 4*

The scores show two students at Basic level, five students at Level 1, four students at Level 2, and one student at Level 3.

Student	Test score (# correct)	Student's Book level
Student #1	12	1
Student #2	2	Basic
Student #3	14	2
Student #4	25	3
Student #5	5	1
Student #6	3	Basic
Student #7	18	2
Student #8	11	1
Student #9	8	1
Student #10	10	1
Student #11	21	2
Student #12	16	2

This correlation will help determine the number of like-ability groups in the class and how many different levels of *Ventures* are needed. A teacher who wants no more than three like-ability groups might put Student #4, who tested at a Level 3, with the Level 2 students, and therefore have only three levels: Basic, 1, and 2. A teacher who wants only two like-ability groups might put the Basic and Level 1 students into one group, thereby having only Levels 1 and 2.

Monitoring progress

In addition to using assessments to place students and to guide instruction, teachers also need assessments that monitor progress. In the multilevel classroom, monitoring progress can be especially challenging since it involves checking the progress of students at different proficiency levels. The *Ventures* series provides several different tools for assessing student progress – self-assessments, review lessons, tests, and projects.

Self-assessments At the end of each unit, students complete a self-assessment found in the back of the level-appropriate Student's Book. The self-assessments are an important part of students' learning and success. They give students an opportunity to evaluate and reflect on their learning and decide if they are ready to take the unit test.

Review lessons After every two units, there is a review lesson. The review lessons recycle, reinforce, and consolidate the language presented in the previous two units and include a pronunciation activity.

Tests For each unit there is a unit test. These tests assess listening, grammar, reading, and writing, with real-life documents incorporated into the reading and writing sections. Hard copies of the tests, as well as the answer key and audio script, are in the Teacher's Edition. The audio program for the tests is on the Teacher's Toolkit Audio CD / CD-ROM in the Teacher's Edition. The Teacher's Edition also has a midterm test, covering Units 1–5, and a final test, covering Units 6–10.

Projects Each unit has a project at the back of the Student's Book. In the projects, students either develop a product or perform an Internet search. Projects provide a culminating activity for students to synthesize what they have learned. When done collaboratively, projects also help to build a sense of community.

SUMMARY

Ventures addresses level-specific and non level-specific multilevel classes. Because of *Add Ventures*, the *Ventures* series is well suited to the level-specific class. Because of the commonalities across the different levels of the Student's Books and Workbooks, the *Ventures* series is equally suited for the non level-specific class. A placement test helps teachers assign students to level-appropriate books, and tools for monitoring progress (unit tests, midterm and final tests, and the self-assessments), as well as review lessons and projects, provide additional resources for multilevel teachers.

Chapter 3 describes the *Ventures* Multilevel Organizers and discusses how to use them to simplify multilevel class management and save on preparation time.

The Ventures Multilevel Organizers

How do you manage multiple proficiency levels within one class?

As described in Chapter 2, the *Ventures* series is designed so that different levels of Student's Books and Workbooks can be used easily within multilevel classrooms.

This chapter describes another way in which the *Ventures* series simplifies teaching in the non level-specific class. The *Ventures* Multilevel Organizers and CD-ROM in this Planner help teachers to (1) use *Ventures* to group students in one-class classrooms, (2) recognize what teaching steps to take for each lesson in *Ventures*, and (3) determine which *Ventures* books and which parts of the lesson to assign to like-ability groups.

This chapter shows how the *Ventures* Multilevel Organizers also relate the underlying principles of successful multilevel instruction.

This chapter presents:

• an overview of the *Ventures* Multilevel Organizers
• grouping strategies in the *Ventures* Multilevel Organizers
• ways to support the *Ventures* Multilevel Organizers with the CD-ROM
• ways to adapt the *Ventures* Multilevel Organizers

Overview of the Ventures Multilevel Organizers

Using the Organizers can significantly reduce class preparation time. Their purpose is two-fold: (1) to highlight grouping strategies and (2) to suggest teaching steps. There are two sets of organizers, one for each purpose.

The Multilevel Organizers: At-a-Glance The Multilevel Organizers: At-a-Glance is the set of Organizers that highlights grouping strategies. Turn to page 17 to see an example of the At-a-Glance Organizer for Lesson A. The At-a-Glance Organizers illustrate classroom management and indicate whether the teacher or a group leader facilitates or students work independently. The Organizers also identify objectives and materials and provide a place for the teacher to assign time allotments for each part of the class.

The Multilevel Organizers: Teaching Steps The Multilevel Organizers: Teaching Steps are more detailed than the At-a Glance Organizers, offering specific instructions for teacher-directed, whole-group opening and closing activities and for each break-out time with like-ability groups. They also give teachers a place to indicate the *Ventures* books used at each proficiency level (low, mid, high). Turn to pages 18–20 to see an example of the Teaching Steps Organizer for Lesson A.

Each set of the Multilevel Organizers – the At-a-Glance and the Teaching Steps – has six separate Organizers, one for each of the six lesson types in the *Ventures* series. These lesson types are:

Lesson A – Get ready (Vocabulary and Listening)
Lesson B – Vocabulary (Basic) or Grammar (Books 1–4)
Lesson C – Grammar
Lesson D – Reading
Lesson E – Writing
Lesson F – Another view (Life-skills literacy)

The At-a-Glance and Teaching Step Organizers can be used for the specific lesson in all units and in all levels of the *Ventures* series used in the class. Teachers can also personalize or adapt them for their own classes.

Assumptions for using the Organizers

The Organizers assume the following conditions in the class:

• a division of each class into three main time periods
  – two-thirds of class time spent in like-ability groups
  – one-third of class time spent on opening and closing whole-class or cross-ability activities
• three proficiency levels of students within the class (grouped as low, mid, high)
• appropriate levels of *Ventures* Student Books, Workbooks, Teacher's Editions, and class CDs or cassettes for each of the three levels
• group leaders to assist groups that are not working with the teacher

Grouping strategies on the Multilevel Organizers

An important part of multilevel lesson planning is determining when to have students work in whole groups and when to have them work in like-ability groups. A common approach in many multilevel classrooms is to start and finish with the whole group and break out with like-ability groups during the middle of the class. The chart below illustrates that management strategy and shows the purpose for each grouping.

<table>
<tr><td>

Opening activities: whole group

Objective: Build community and introduce unit theme or focus on skill / lesson

</td></tr>
</table>

<table>
<tr><td>

Break-out activities: like-ability groups

Objective: Develop level-appropriate language skills

</td></tr>
</table>

<table>
<tr><td>

Closing activities: whole group

Objective: Assess learning from break-out groups

</td></tr>
</table>

Whole-group activities

Teacher-facilitated whole-group activities are extremely important in a multilevel class. On the Organizers, the teacher opens and closes each class with whole-group activities. These whole-group activities build community and emphasize collaboration. Students negotiate meaning, take risks, have fun, and understand they are part of a supportive learning community. The activities assure students that the teacher is leading the class; they promote learning from each other and build confidence that all proficiency levels will be addressed; and they allow students to demonstrate their abilities in a non-threatening, carefully structured atmosphere.

Opening whole-group activities The opening whole-group activities introduce a unit theme or introduce the language skill (listening, speaking, reading, writing, grammar, vocabulary, or life-skills literacy) that is the focus of the lesson. Some opening whole-group activities included in the Organizers are:

• **Responding to visuals:** Students talk about what they see in a big picture or in a sequence of pictures. They identify vocabulary, and they develop and role-play conversations involving the characters in the picture.

• **Storytelling based on picture sequences:** Students talk about a sequence of pictures, working together to tell a story, predict what will happen, or identify a problem. Using the language experience approach, teachers can use the information from students to write a story about the picture.

• **Reading life-skills literacy documents:** Students scan a document for information. The teacher asks questions about the document's features (heading, format, key points), and then students answer questions about the form, chart, or graph.

Closing whole-group activities The closing whole-group activities focus on reviewing and assessing student learning. Often they include cross-ability groups in which students at different ability levels work together, enabling peer teaching and peer correction.

Some closing whole-group activities are:

• **Student projects:** At the back of each level of the *Ventures* Student's Books, there are ten projects, one for each unit. Completing projects integrates assessment, requires the use of multiple language skills, and builds community as students focus on a shared interest and collaborate meaningfully.

• **Gallery walks:** Students post their writing samples from the break-out groups. All students walk around, read the writing samples, and respond to questions. This activity provides students with an opportunity to read and share writings with classmates. Students at a higher proficiency level can help students at a lower level understand the higher-level writing, thereby encouraging peer teaching and offering another opportunity for community building.

• **Self-assessments:** Students use the self-assessments at the back of each level of the Student's Books to identify key vocabulary and review vocabulary with other students in the class. In this activity, all students act as peer tutors and learners.

Break-out time in like-ability groups

Teaching the non level-specific class is most successful when classes can be broken into two or more like-ability groups using level-appropriate Student's Books. If there are two proficiency levels in the class, the teacher creates two like-ability groups, each using a different level of *Ventures.* If there are three proficiency levels, there are three like-ability groups using three different levels of *Ventures*. Which *Ventures* Student's Books are used for these groups depends on the proficiency levels of students.

Determining number of like-ability groups

The *Ventures* Multilevel Organizers refer to the like-ability groups as low-, mid-, and high-level rather than beginning, intermediate, and advanced. The following examples illustrate why.

Scenario #1

This class has students who are at the proficiency levels of *Ventures* Basic, 1, and 2. In this case, students using *Ventures* Basic would be the low-level group, students using *Ventures* Level 1 would be the mid-level group, and students using *Ventures* Level 2 would be the high-level group.

Scenario #2

This class has students who are at the proficieny levels of *Ventures* 2, 3, and 4. In this case, students using *Ventures* Level 2 would be the low-level group, the mid-level group would be students using *Ventures* Level 3, and the high-level group would be the students using *Ventures* Level 4.

The following table summarizes these two scenarios.

Scenario	Low-level	Mid-level	High-level
Scenario #1	*Ventures* Basic	*Ventures* 1	*Ventures* 2
Scenario #2	*Ventures* 2	*Ventures* 3	*Ventures* 4

Three groups is a common and useful division in multilevel classrooms. However, there are also classes in which teachers use two groups or more than three groups. Whether a teacher creates two, three, or four proficiency groups and selects corresponding level-appropriate books will depend on one or more of the following factors:

- **The length of the class.** Each student group expects the teacher to work with the group during each class period. In classes of less than two hours, this may not be possible if there are many groups.
- **The number of students in the class.** Activities in each like-ability group encourage student interaction. If there are fewer than four students, opportunities for such interaction may be limited. In such cases, a teacher may choose to put students at two different proficiency levels in the same group.
- **The resources for managing like-ability groups.** Teachers without an aide or who are uncomfortable with student group leaders or with having students work independently will probably want fewer groups.

- **The teacher's own experience and comfort level with multiple-level groups.** Teachers who have limited experience or are uncomfortable with managing several groups within one class will probably be more successful initially with only two groups.

Arranging the classroom for like-ability groups

Creating like-ability groups also means designing the classroom to allow for the transition between whole group and multiple-leveled groups. Different parts of the classroom can be designated for different like-ability groups. For example, if the seating arrangement is u-shaped, each portion of the "u" can be a different group of students – one "side" of the "u" for one group, the bottom of the "u" for a second group, and the other side of the "u" for a third group.

If the seating arrangement is rows of individual student desk-chairs, the desks can be clustered into three different corners of the room.

Grouping like-ability students together for their break-out time encourages interaction and collaboration and is an effective support for students when their teacher is not facilitating their group.

The teacher's role and responsibilities

The break-out time provides like-ability groups an opportunity to work together on level-appropriate material. When there are multiple groups working simultaneously, the teacher will be with only one of those groups at a time.

The Organizers direct teacher movement from group to group for break-out times. The teacher's time with each break-out group focuses on presentation. It also includes setting up the tasks to be completed when the teacher is not with the group and directing follow-up tasks with Group Leaders.

The teacher should always begin with the low-level group because that group will need the most guidance. However, before presenting to the low-level group, the teacher needs to check with the other groups to be sure they understand the tasks and are using the correct materials. It is best to check with the highest group first since that group should be able to work independently more easily. Then the teacher spends the first break-out time with the low-level group, the second break-out time with the mid-level group, and the third break-out time with the high-level group.

Whenever students are given break-out group work, the teacher must make it clear that the lesson is always teacher-guided, that there will be follow-up with the teacher on all tasks, and that there will be whole-group opportunities for review after the break-out time. If this is not made clear, students will lose interest in doing the work and will feel that they are not learning.

Here are a few ways a teacher can manage break-out group work:

Set time limits. Clearly identify, orally and in writing, how long students will be working in like-ability groups and when they will reconvene with the teacher. One way to do this is to distribute a copy of the Break-out Organizer to each group. At the end of each break-out time, the teacher should clarify the tasks and time line for each group before leading the next group.

Identify materials. Post the materials to be used during the break-out time. Identify the materials by book, unit, lesson, and page number(s) (e.g., Student Book 2, Unit 1, Lesson A, page 6).

Select a group leader. Choose a student leader from within each group. The leader facilitates activities that require interaction among participants in the group and serves as a timekeeper, moving students from one activity to the next. The student leader can record questions that group members have and ensure that they are presented to the teacher for clarification.

Follow up with groups working without a teacher. Do a spot check to review the work just completed in small groups. Have the group identify items within exercises where they had problems, and review those items with the group. Elicit and answer questions that students have as a result of the activities.

Group leaders

When the teacher is not working with a group, it can be very helpful to have someone else be responsible for facilitating the group. The facilitator can be (1) an instructional aide or outside volunteer or (2) a student leader.

An instructional aide or volunteer A group leader from outside the class might be an instructional aide, a student teacher, or a volunteer from the community. It is important that the group leader have an opportunity to preview the materials before facilitating the group and an opportunity to ask the teacher any questions that come up as a result of that preview. Minimally, this group leader should have a list of steps for facilitation and a set of materials with answers.

The *Ventures* series makes it easy for an aide or volunteer with little preparation to help with break-out groups because:

• detailed teaching instructions for each lesson are in the level-appropriate Teacher's Edition;

• answers to exercises are included on the reproduced Student's Book pages in the Teacher's Editions;

• answers to Workbook exercises are included in the back of the Workbook;

• the audio scripts for all listening exercises are included in the Teacher's Editions and on the CD-ROM at the back of this *Planner*.

A student leader Many multilevel teachers will not have an instructional aide or volunteer to help in the classroom. In that case, a student leader can be a powerful resource to support group work.

Using students as group leaders emphasizes one of the most important tenets for learning: The best way to learn is to teach. Because explaining and demonstrating information promotes student learning and self-confidence, rotating the job of group leader among students is an effective instructional process as well as a management tool. As long as the student feels prepared and supported, using students as group leaders can be very effective in the multilevel classroom.

A student group leader may be a student at a higher level assisting a lower-level group or a student facilitating his / her own group. When a higher-level student leader is with a lower-level group, the teacher first presents and models the tasks. Then, after the teacher has moved to another group, the student leader facilitates exercises. Facilitation can include assigning partners for pair work, moving students from one exercise to another, and using answer keys to check work.

Student leaders from within a group are most common, and most effective, with the mid- and high-level groups. Facilitation can include posting the agenda for the break-out time and eliciting and recording questions students want to ask the teacher when he / she facilitates the group's break-out time.

When the student leader is assisting a group other than his / her own, it is important that the teacher provide a means for that student to pick up the learning that occurred within his / her own group. For example, the student leader could partner with another student who is in the same level, do activities missed in class as homework, or meet with the teacher on a one-on-one basis.

Materials to support independent study

Using materials that minimize student dependency on the teacher is one way to free the teacher to concentrate on one group while others work independently. The Organizers include break-out times where independent work is an option. For students working in groups without a teacher or group leader, the *Ventures* student materials incorporate features that support this independent study. These include:

Audio program The audio program provides a clear model and answers to activities marked with the audio icon in the Student's Book. Each Student's Book has an self-study audio CD and transcripts for those listening exercises. There is also a class audio program with all recorded material for the Student's Book. A complete transcript of the class audio program is in the Teacher's Edition and on the CD-ROM at the back of this *Planner*. Both the transcript and answer key can be copied for students to use for self-correction. Students in one group can, therefore, use the audio independently during the break-out time while the teacher works with another group.

The Workbook The *Ventures* Workbooks include grammar charts related to the grammar activities and answer keys for each exercise. Using materials that have clear directions and answer keys can reduce the need for the teacher to set up each activity, enabling students to work independently and check their answers. Their time with the teacher can be spent on only those items that they have misunderstood.

Predictable structure and clear directions As described in Chapter 2, the lessons within *Ventures* follow the same predictable order across books, units, and levels. The activities within the same lessons follow the same sequencing across levels and units. Directions are simple, and, when appropriate, the answer for the first item in an exercise is filled in, serving as an example. This predictability is very supportive of independent study.

Delineating like-ability group tasks

It is important for students, volunteers, and instructional aides to have a clear understanding of what is expected of them while they facilitate their break-out time groups. Teachers can make this clear by:
• posting the list of tasks and materials for the tasks on a wall near the group with a suggested time frame to complete the tasks;
• completing the blank Multilevel Organizer templates on pages 41–44 or on the CD-ROM at the back of this *Planner*, and distributing them to groups to guide the tasks for the break-out time;
• copying and distributing audio scripts from the CD-ROM in this *Planner* and answer keys from the Teacher's Edition to encourage peer correction.

CD-ROM with Organizers

The CD-ROM in the back of this Planner includes color visuals, class audio scripts, the Multilevel Organizer: At-a-Glance for each of the six lesson types, the Multilevel Organizer: Teaching Steps for each of the six lesson types, and the Multilevel Lesson Plan Templates.

Color visuals

There are 21 color visuals from various levels of the Student's Books. For each of the ten units in the Student's Books, there are two visuals – Picture A is one of the opening pictures in Lesson A taken from Student's Books Basic, 1, and 2; Picture B is one of the picture sequences in Lesson A taken from Student's Books 3 and 4. There is also a color visual for the opening picture in the Welcome unit, which is the same visual in all five levels. These visuals were selected because they offered the broadest possibility of language exploitation regardless of proficiency level of students in the class.

These visuals are a resource for the whole-class activities in the Organizers. They can be printed and made into transparencies for use with overhead projectors; they can also be printed and distributed so that each student in the class has a copy. The visuals can also be projected on a large screen using an LCD projector.

The following chart identifies the Student's Books from which the visuals are drawn and units for which they are recommended.

Unit	Picture A	Picture B
1	*Ventures* 1	*Ventures* 3
2	*Ventures* Basic	*Ventures* 3
3	*Ventures* Basic	*Ventures* 3
4	*Ventures* 1	*Ventures* 3
5	*Ventures* 1	*Ventures* 3
6	*Ventures* Basic	*Ventures* 4
7	*Ventures* 2	*Ventures* 4
8	*Ventures* 1	*Ventures* 4
9	*Ventures* 2	*Ventures* 3
10	*Ventures* Basic	*Ventures* 4

Audio scripts

The CD-ROM has photocopiable audio scripts for all of the listening activities in the *Ventures* Student's Books as well as for the unit tests. The scripts can be copied and distributed to students to help them make connections between oral and written language. Students can also use them to self-correct exercises. In addition, group leaders can use them to guide corrections within like-ability and cross-ability groups.

Multilevel Organizer: At-a-Glance and Multilevel Organizer: Teaching Steps

The Organizers are included on the CD-ROM so that they can be easily printed and made into transparencies for use with overhead projectors; they can also be printed and distributed so that each student or group leader can have a copy to guide the teaching and management of the class. The Organizers can also be projected on a large screen using an LCD projector.

Multilevel Lesson Plan Templates

The purpose of the photocopiable templates is to assist teachers in creating their own individualized lesson plans. They mirror the At-a-Glance and Teaching Steps Organizers, but they include blanks for teachers to fill in information about their own classes and lessons.

Adapting the Organizers

The Organizers incorporate the approach to multilevel instruction described in the earlier chapters of this *Multilevel Lesson Planner*. However, as each class offers a different challenge and each teacher has his / her own way of addressing those challenges, there will be a need and desire to adapt. This last section includes suggestions for ways in which the Organizers can be adapted to different approaches.

Adapting the number of break-out groups

The Organizers assume three break-out groups. However, the Organizers can be adapted to include fewer or more like-ability groups.

Adapting the lesson sequence for break-out times

As described above, the Organizers assume that during each break-out time, students will work on the same lesson in their level-appropriate *Ventures* Student's Book and Workbook during the same time. That is, if the low-level group is working on Lesson A, the mid- and high-level groups are also working on Lesson A. This enables the teacher to focus opening and closing activities on the same topic and language skills.

However, some teachers may prefer to have different break-out groups work on different lessons at the same time. For example, the low-level break-out group may work on Lesson A while the mid-level break-out group works on Lesson D and the high-level break-out group

works on Lesson B or C. In a classroom where the teacher does not have an instructional aide or volunteer and chooses not to designate a student leader, assigning lessons that need less teacher attention to one or two groups may allow the teacher more time for presentation and practice with another group.

Adapting the amount of time with each break-out group

The Organizers assume equal amounts of break-out time in each lesson with each group. Some teachers may, however, want to vary the amount of time with each group. For example, a teacher may spend more time with the low-level group during each lesson and less time with the mid- and high-level groups. Or, the teacher many want to spend more time with certain groups for certain lessons. For example, a teacher may want to dedicate more time to high-level groups during Lessons B and C and less teacher time during Lessons D and E. Another variation is to spend more time with the group that has the largest number of students and less time with the group that has the smallest number of students.

Adapting different activities for different parts of the lesson

Each Teaching Steps Organizer identifies specific activities for opening, break-out groups, and closing. You may want to change or omit some of these activities.

SUMMARY

With the Organizers in hand, teachers can enter the classroom with the confidence of knowing *how* to group students, *what* teaching steps to take, and *which* books and *which* parts of the lesson to assign to groups. The Organizers help teachers meet the challenges of the multilevel classroom and significantly reduce preparation time.

Chapter 4 describes other *Ventures* resources and suggests how teachers might go beyond the Student's Books and Workbooks and use a wider variety of appropriate materials in the multilevel classroom.

How can other *Ventures* resources be used in the multilevel classroom?

The *Ventures* Multilevel Organizers, as described in Chapter 3, provide a blueprint for delivering effective multilevel instruction using *Ventures* Student's Books and Workbooks. The purpose of this chapter is to highlight additional *Ventures* resources that enhance multilevel instruction.

This chapter focuses on resources in the following *Ventures* components:
• Student's Books
• Teacher's Edition and Teacher's Toolkit CD-ROM
• *Ventures* Web site, Student Arcade, and TestCrafter

Student's Books

Each level of the Student's Book has three features for enriching the multilevel classroom experience: a self-study audio CD, projects, and review lessons.

Self-study audio CD

The self-study audio CD includes the listening for selected activities identified by this icon [icon]. The CD is in the back of each Student's Book, and the track number, correlated to the page and exercise, is on the inside back cover. The self-study audio is an especially useful tool in situations where a class takes place in, or has access to, a language lab, as well as in situations where there is a room adjacent to the classroom. It enables students to listen to the materials on their own. It can also be used effectively in break-out groups without a group leader and at learning stations.

The self-study audio CD is an invaluable tool for encouraging students to take responsibility for their own learning, enabling those who want or need to review materials to do so independently.

Projects

For each unit in the Student's Book there is one project. The project reinforces the topic / themes and language in the unit. Located in the back of the Student's Book, the projects provide directions for students to gather information from an Internet search or another source; and report information by producing a poster, time line, or another product. In the final step of each project, students share their information.

Projects can be done independently either outside of class or during break-out times in place of Workbook exercises. Workbook exercises, then, can be assigned as

homework. Whether done outside of class or in class in place of Workbook exercises, there should always be a time for students to report back to the whole class.

Projects are also an effective way to provide closure to a unit and, as such, can replace the closing activity in the Lesson F Multilevel Organizer. Each like-ability group can do the project for its level and share the projects through a gallery walk. Projects can also be done in cross-ability groups; the teacher can create small groups with one student from each level in each group and assign different students different roles. For example, one student might do the research, another record the answers, and a third report back to the class.

Review lessons

Review lessons have exercises that focus on listening, grammar, and pronunciation. They appear after every two units in the Student's Book. The listening and pronunciation portions of the review lessons are included on the Class Audio CD; however, these activities are not CD-dependent, as all of the audio scripts are printed in the Teacher's Edition and on the CD-ROM at the back of this *Planner*. Teachers without means to play the CD can read aloud from the audio scripts.

The review lessons can also become a closing activity in the Lesson F Multilevel Organizer. Students can do the grammar, listening, or pronunciation portions of the lesson independently, and at listening stations (i.e., playback equipment with headsets or earphones). By providing students with the answers on the Student's Book page in the Teacher's Edition, the teacher can also encourage students to self-correct or peer correct.

Teacher's Edition resources

The *Ventures* Teacher's Edition provides step-by-step teaching notes for each lesson and answers. It also includes the script for the class audio, tests, games, and the Teacher's Toolkit Audio CD / CD-ROM.

Teaching notes and exercise answers

The teaching notes in the *Ventures* Teacher's Edition are presented side-by-side with the corresponding Student's Book page. The notes are organized by the stages of a lesson: warm-up and review, presentation, practice, comprehension check, application, and evaluation. They also provide teaching tips, culture notes, expansion activities, and suggestions for promoting learner persistence and community building. The interleaved pages from the Student's Book include the answers.

In addition, the teaching notes and answer keys are especially useful for teachers who are working with a group leader. Depending on the group leader's responsibilities, the teacher can provide the leader with the teaching notes, the Student's Book pages with the answer keys, or both. By providing the group leader with these resources, the teacher reduces the time needed to spend preparing the group leader. If there is no group leader, the teacher can reproduce the Student's Book pages with answers and put them in a folder so students can check their answers independently.

Script for the Class Audio CDs / cassettes

The script for the Class Audio enables a teacher to conduct listening activities without relying on technology. Moreover, by providing students with a copy of the script, the teacher enables students to review the audio and self-check comprehension. The audio scripts are available on the CD-ROM at the back of this Planner and at the back of each Teacher's Edition.

Tests

At the back of the Teacher's Editions are reproducible test pages, the scripts for the audio portion of the tests, and the answer keys. The tests and the audio portion of the tests are also on the Teacher's Toolkit Audio CD / CD-ROM so that teachers can download and print them. There is a test for each unit, and each test includes four sections: listening, grammar, reading, and writing. There is also a midterm test, which covers Units 1–5, and a final test, which covers Units 6–10.

These tests provide a tool for teachers to monitor student progress and document gains. Teachers can have all students take the test for their level at the same time as a closing activity for a unit. Another option is for the teacher to have different groups take the test at different times; students in one group can take the test while the teacher reviews materials with another group not yet ready for the test.

Games

An overview for various games is available in the Additional Resources section of each Teacher's Edition. It identifies the skill focus, the objective, and the preparation required for each game in addition to step-by-step directions. Some of the games are: Stand By, Picture It, and Disappearing Dialog.

Games are a fun and engaging way to motivate students. They are especially effective in whole-group

and cross-ability groups during opening and closing activities. Any of the games can replace the suggested opening or closing activities in the Multilevel Organizers.

Teacher's Toolkit resources

The Teacher's Toolkit is an audio CD / CD-ROM included in the back of each Teacher's Edition. It includes Collaborative Activities, Picture Dictionary cards, Extended Reading Worksheets, tests, vocabulary lists, real-life documents, and a certificate of completion. It includes more than 200 pages of additional material, some of which is described below.

Collaborative Activity Worksheets

Collaborative Activities are designed to reinforce the skills of a lesson. They provide additional practice with the skill but are less structured and more communicative. There is one Collaborative Activity Worksheet for each lesson in each unit, making a total of 60 per Student's Book. Some of the Collaborative Activities are:

- **Find the differences.** Students work in pairs, comparing two similar but different pictures.
- **Unscramble.** Students arrange sentences into a sequence to create a story.
- **Student interview.** Students interview classmates and report back on the information they gather.

Collaborative Activities are especially effective in cross-ability groups. As such, they can replace the closing activity suggested in the Multilevel Organizer. They can also be used in like-ability groups as additional practice if students finish their group activity before other groups have finished.

Picture Dictionary Cards and Worksheets

There is one set of reproducible picture cards for each unit in *Ventures* Basic, 1, and 2. The pictures are the same as those in the Picture Dictionary in Lesson D of the Student's Book. The cards help to clarify meaning and provide a tool for kinesthetic learners. The flash cards themselves are letter size (8½ x 11), but they can be printed in smaller sizes with more than one to a page. The *Ventures* Teacher Support Site (www.cambridge.org/ventures) provides directions on how to print multiple cards on one sheet of paper. The Teacher's Toolkit Audio CD / CD-ROM includes suggestions on how to use the cards, games to play, and a worksheet that reinforces the vocabulary for each set of cards.

The flash cards can encourage cross-ability interaction as a closing activity in the Lesson D Multilevel Organizer; the teacher can form small groups, one student from each level in the group, and students in each group can share and "teach" the words on their picture cards to others in their group. Flash card games can also provide a fun and engaging way to close out a unit.

For each set of flash cards there is an accompanying worksheet. These worksheets are an appropriate replacement for the **Communicate** activity that accompanies the Picture Dictionary in the Student's Book when students need more reading and writing practice. The worksheets can also be used at the beginning of class for review, and they can provide yet another way for like-ability groups during the break-out time to practice when they finish activities earlier than other groups. Teachers could have worksheet folders, and students could access these materials when time allows.

Extended Reading Worksheets

There is one Extended Reading Worksheet for each unit in *Ventures* Student's Books 3 and 4. The worksheets provide an additional high-interest reading on the unit-related topic. Designed to take 15 to 30 minutes, they reinforce skills introduced in the Student's Book, expand vocabulary-building strategies, and encourage critical thinking. The Teacher's Toolkit Audio CD / CD-ROM includes directions on how to prepare the materials and how to use the worksheets.

In the multilevel class, the extended reading worksheet can replace the reading in Lesson D of the Student's Book for like-ability group work, and the reading in Lesson D can be assigned as homework; it can also be added to the in-class break-out time for Lesson D. Another option is to use it as an optional activity for students to do when they complete activities early or outside of class.

Real-life Documents

The *Ventures* Teacher's Toolkit Audio CD / CD-ROM for Basic and Levels 1 and 2 contains ten reproducible Real-life Documents that are forms to be completed. Some of the forms are a version of the document in Lesson F of the Student's Book; some are versions that are new to the students but that review an earlier unit presentation (e.g., a classmate description form).

These forms can provide additional like-ability, cross-ability, and whole-class practice. For like-ability group practice, students can complete forms with information about themselves or a partner. The teacher can also have students complete the forms as homework or as a replacement for the Workbook activity. For a closing activity, the teacher can have students report back orally to the whole class about their partner or have students post their completed forms so that students can do a gallery walk, reading each other's work.

Ventures and technology

The *Ventures* Web site (www.cambridge.org/ventures) provides a wealth of material for those with access to the Internet. The Web site includes the *Ventures* Student Arcade, Teacher's Toolkit (as described on page 15), Placement Test (as described in Chapter 2), Correlations to State and National Standards and Benchmarks, the Self-study audio, and the Canadian Teacher's Guide.

The *Ventures* Student Arcade is a student support site (www.cambridge.org/us/esl/venturesarcade) that provides students with additional self-access practice with the language in *Ventures*. There is a Student Arcade for each unit of the five levels in the *Ventures* series. The game-like activities provide practice with listening, vocabulary, grammar, and reading.

In the multilevel classroom with access to computers and the Internet, the Student Arcade provides effective extension activities for like-ability break-out groups. The arcade activities can also be a substitute for the Workbook activities. Teachers can provide the Web address to students so that they can do independent practice outside of class or in computer labs.

Ventures TestCrafter is a test generator CD-ROM that allows teachers to create, edit, and print tests for each unit of all five levels of *Ventures*. The tests can also be loaded onto the Internet for students to take the tests on their own computers.

Teachers can use ready-made tests, or they can draw from a bank of 2,000 multiple-choice questions. They can edit the questions or add questions to create customized tests.

The flexibility of TestCrafter enables teachers of multilevel classes to create unit or skills tests with varying levels of difficulty to match proficiency levels that are in the class.

Summary

Ventures offers a complete package of support materials for teachers as they identify needs not covered solely by Student's Books and Workbooks. As time and comfort permit, teachers will want to experiment with additional supplemental activities outlined in this chapter.

Multilevel teachers no longer need to spend hours developing their own student materials. Teachers can use their valuable time to select existing materials that are engaging and relevant and that promote student success.

Multilevel Organizer: At-a-glance

Opening activities: whole group	Opening activities
Objective Build community and introduce unit theme **Materials** Picture A (on CD-ROM) **Activity** Build vocabulary	☐ Minutes

Break-out activities: like-ability groups

Objective
Develop level-appropriate language skills

Low-level	Mid-level	High-level	
Facilitator `Teacher` **Materials** Student's Book Lesson A	**Facilitator** Group Leader **Materials** Student's Book and audio Lesson A	**Facilitator** Independent **Materials** Workbook Lesson A	**Break-out: Time 1** ☐ Minutes
Facilitator Group Leader **Materials** Workbook Lesson A	**Facilitator** `Teacher` **Materials** Student's Book and Workbook Lesson A	**Facilitator** Independent **Materials** Student's Book and audio Lesson A	**Break-out: Time 2** ☐ Minutes
Facilitator Group Leader **Materials** Student's Book and audio Lesson A	**Facilitator** Independent **Materials** Workbook Lesson A	**Facilitator** `Teacher` **Materials** Student's Book Lesson A	**Break-out: Time 3** ☐ Minutes

Closing activities: whole group and cross-ability groups	Closing activities
Objective Assess learning from break-out groups **Materials** Student's Books from each level **Activity** Review vocabulary	☐ Minutes

Multilevel Organizer: Teaching steps

Low-level: Book _____	Mid-level: Book _____	High-level: Book _____

Opening activities: whole group

Objective Build community and introduce unit theme or vocabulary

Facilitator Teacher

Materials Picture A (on CD-ROM)

Activity Build vocabulary

Teaching steps

1. **T** asks, "What do you see?"
2. **Ss** identify what they see in the picture.
   - Low-level **Ss** respond with words and phrases.
   - Higher-level **Ss** use sentences.
3. **T** writes vocabulary on the board.
4. **T** does one or more of the following:
   - **Ss** say words and **T** points to items in picture.
   - **Ss** ask and answer questions about the picture.
   - **Ss** say words, and other **Ss** circle the words on the board.

Break-out activities: like-ability groups (see next page)

Closing activities: whole group

Objective Assess learning from break-out groups

Facilitator Teacher

Materials Student's Books from each level

Activity Review vocabulary

Teaching steps

1. **T** does one or more of following:
   - **Ss** from each group write key level-appropriate vocabulary on board.
   - **Ss** ask whole group to identify / pronounce words.
   - **Ss** in higher groups help **Ss** in lower groups pronounce / identify words in the lower-level **Ss** books.
2. **Ss** from each group come to the board. **T** names a letter of the alphabet. **Ss** write one or more words from their Student's Book that begin with that letter.

Abbreviations used in the organizers

T = teacher   GL = group leader: instructional aide, volunteer, student leader
S = student   Ss = students
Picture A = unit-opening picture from Student's Books Basic, 1, or 2
Picture B = unit-opening picture from Student's Books 3 or 4
1A/2B (any boldfaced numbers and letters) = reference to exercises in the Student's Books

Break-out activities: like-ability groups

Objective Develop level-appropriate language skills

Break-out: Time 1

Low-level	Mid-level	High-level
Facilitator Teacher **Materials** Low-level Student's Book and Workbook **Teaching steps** 1. **T** focuses **Ss** on opening picture in **1 Talk**. 2. Review vocabulary. 3. **T** models pronunciation of key vocabulary. 4. **Ss** identify and pronounce key vocabulary. 5. **Ss** point to and discuss people / things in the picture. 6. **T** introduces Lesson A in the Workbook.	**Facilitator** Group Leader **Materials** Mid-level Student's Book and audio **Teaching steps** 1. **GL** introduces **2A** and plays audio. 2. **Ss** complete exercise. 3. **GL** checks answers using audio script or Teacher's Edition answer key. 4. **GL** reads directions for **2B** and plays audio. 5. **Ss** complete exercise. 6. **GL** checks answers using Teacher's Edition answer key. 7. **Ss** continue until all exercises are completed and checked.	**Facilitator** Independent **Materials** High-level Workbook **Teaching steps** 1. **T** introduces Workbook Lesson A, points out answer key in Workbook, and leaves group to work independently. 2. **Ss** work in pairs or small groups to complete exercises. 3. **Ss** check answers (with answer key, or with partner and then with answer key).

Break-out: Time 2

Low-level	Mid-level	High-level
Facilitator Group Leader **Materials** Low-level Workbook **Teaching steps** 1. **GL** introduces Lesson A. 2. **Ss** work in pairs or small groups to complete Lesson A exercises. 3. **GL** checks answers using answer key in Workbook. 4. **Ss** read answers aloud.	**Facilitator** Teacher **Materials** Mid-level Student's Book and Workbook **Teaching steps** 1. **T** reviews **2 Listening**. 2. **T** facilitates exercises in **1 Talk** and models pronunciation of key vocabulary. 3. **Ss** identify and pronounce key vocabulary. 4. **T** introduces Workbook Lesson A and points out answer key in Workbook.	**Facilitator** Independent **Materials** High-level Student's Book and audio **Teaching steps** 1. **Ss** read directions for **2A**, play audio, and complete exercise. 2. **Ss** check answers using audio script or Teacher's Edition answer key. 3. **Ss** do same for **2B**. If time, **Ss** role-play conversations in **2B**, using audio script at back of the Student's Book.

Low-level	Mid-level	High-level
Facilitator Group Leader	**Facilitator** Independent	**Facilitator** **Teacher**
Materials Low-level Student's Book and audio	**Materials** Mid-level Workbook	**Materials** High-level Student's Book
Teaching steps 1. **GL** reads directions for **2A** and plays the audio. 2. **Ss** complete the exercise. 3. **GL** checks answers using audio script or Teacher's Edition answer key. 4. **GL** does same for **2B**. 5. **GL** and **Ss** continue until all exercises are completed and checked.	**Teaching steps** 1. **Ss** work in pairs or small groups to complete exercises. 2. **Ss** check answers using answer key in Workbook. 3. **Ss** practice reading answers.	**Teaching steps** 1. **T** reviews **2 Listening**. 2. **T** facilitates exercises in **1 Talk** and models pronunciation of key vocabulary. 3. **Ss** identify and pronounce key vocabulary. 4. **T** uses unit grammar to discuss pictures in **1 Talk**. 5. **T** asks questions to expand **Ss'** use of unit vocabulary.

Multilevel Organizer: At-a-glance

Opening activities: whole group	
Objective To build community and introduce vocabulary / grammar **Materials** Picture A (on CD-ROM) **Activity** Preview vocabulary / grammar	**Opening activities** [ ] Minutes

Break-out activities: like-ability groups

Objective
Develop level-appropriate language skills

Low-level	Mid-level	High-level	
Facilitator Teacher **Materials** Student's Book and audio Lesson B	**Facilitator** Group Leader **Materials** Student's Book and audio Lesson B	**Facilitator** Independent **Materials** Student's Book and Workbook Lesson B	**Break-out: Time 1** [ ] Minutes
Facilitator Group Leader **Materials** Student's Book and audio Lesson B	**Facilitator** Teacher **Materials** Student's Book and Workbook Lesson B	**Facilitator** Independent **Materials** Student's Book and audio Lesson B	**Break-out: Time 2** [ ] Minutes
Facilitator Group Leader **Materials** Workbook Lesson B	**Facilitator** Independent **Materials** Workbook Lesson B	**Facilitator** Teacher **Materials** Student's Book Lesson B	**Break-out: Time 3** [ ] Minutes

Closing activities: cross-ability groups	
Objective Assess learning from break-out groups **Materials** Unit-opening picture in Student's Book from each level **Activity** Review vocabulary / grammar	**Closing activities** [ ] Minutes

Multilevel Organizer: Teaching steps

Low-level: Book _____	Mid-level: Book _____	High-level: Book _____

Opening activities: whole group

Objective Build community and introduce vocabulary / grammar

Facilitator Teacher

Materials Picture A (on CD-ROM)

Activity Preview vocabulary / grammar

Teaching steps

1. **T** describes picture using key vocabulary / grammar.
2. **T** asks questions about picture:
   - *Yes / No* questions for low-level **Ss**
   - *Wh-* questions for higher level **Ss**
3. **T** does one or more of the following:
   - **Ss** ask and answer questions about the picture.
   - **Ss** draw pictures of key vocabulary / grammar. Other **Ss** guess things / actions.
   - **Ss** do question / answer line-up activity. Lower-level **Ss** read questions. Higher-level **Ss** answer.

Break-out activities: like-ability groups (see next page)

Closing activities: cross-ability groups

Objective Assess learning from break-out groups

Facilitator Teacher

Materials Student's Books from each group opened to picture at beginning of the unit

Activity Review vocabulary / grammar

Teaching steps

T does one or more of the following:
- **Ss** work in cross-ability groups (one **S** from each group). Low-level **Ss** point to their picture and say and spell words. Higher-level **Ss** show their picture and describe the picture.
- **Ss** write lesson vocabulary (low-level **Ss**) and sentences (higher-level **Ss**).
- **Ss** in higher group help **Ss** in lower groups pronounce / identify words in the lower-level Student's Books.
- **Ss** share information or role-play their conversations in **3 Communicate.**

Abbreviations used in the organizers

T = teacher   GL = group leader: instructional aide, volunteer, student leader

S = student   Ss = students

Picture A = unit-opening picture from Student's Books Basic, 1, or 2

Picture B = unit-opening picture from Student's Books 3 or 4

1A/2B (any boldfaced numbers and letters) = reference to exercises in the Student's Books

Break-out activities: like-ability groups

Objective Develop level-appropriate language skills

Break-out: Time 1

Low-level	Mid-level	High-level
Facilitator **Teacher** **Materials** Low-level Student's Book and audio **Teaching steps** 1. **T** introduces vocabulary or grammar focus. 2. **T** elicits answers for first two items in **2A**. 3. **Ss** complete exercise and **T** checks answers. If time, **Ss** write answers on board. **T** corrects answers. Optional: **T** plays audio for **Ss** using Student's Book. **Ss** check answers.	**Facilitator** Group Leader **Materials** Mid-level Student's Book and audio **Teaching steps** 1. **Ss** study **1 Grammar focus**. 2. **Ss** complete **2A**. 3. **GL** or **Ss** check answers using audio or Teacher's Edition answer key. 4. **Ss** read answers in pairs or small groups.	**Facilitator** Independent **Materials** High-level Student's Book and Workbook **Teaching steps** 1. **T** introduces Workbook Lesson B, points out answer key in Workbook, and leaves group to work independently. 2. **Ss** study **1 Grammar focus** in Student's Book. 3. **Ss** work in pairs or small groups to complete Lesson B in the Workbook. 4. **Ss** check answers (with Workbook answer key, or with partner and then with answer key).

Break-out: Time 2

Low-level	Mid-level	High-level
Facilitator Group Leader **Materials** Low-level Student's Book **Teaching steps** 1. **GL** reads directions for **2B**. 2. **Ss** complete the exercises. **GL** checks answers using Teacher's Edition answer key. 3. **Ss** complete and check all exercises in **2**. 4. **GL** introduces **3**. **Ss** complete all exercises.	**Facilitator** **Teacher** **Materials** Mid-level Student's Book and Workbook **Teaching steps** 1. **T** reviews **2A**. 2. **T** introduces **2B**. 3. **Ss** complete **2B** and **T** checks answers. 4. **T** introduces **3**. **Ss** complete all exercises in **3**. 5. **T** introduces Workbook Lesson B and points out answer key in Workbook.	**Facilitator** Independent **Materials** High-level Student's Book and audio **Teaching steps** 1. **Ss** review **1 Grammar focus**. 2. **Ss** complete **2A**. 3. **Ss** check answers and practice with a partner. Optional: **Ss** play audio and check answers.

Break-out: Time 3

Low-level	Mid-level	High-level
Facilitator Group Leader	**Facilitator** Independent	**Facilitator** Teacher
Materials Low-level Workbook	**Materials** Mid-level Workbook	**Materials** High-level Student's Book
Teaching steps 1. **GL** introduces Lesson B. 2. **Ss** work in pairs or small groups to complete Lesson B. 3. **GL** checks answers using answer key in the Workbook. 4. **Ss** read answers aloud.	**Teaching steps** 1. **Ss** work in pairs or small groups to complete Lesson B. 2. **Ss** check answers using answer key in Workbook. 3. **Ss** practice reading answers aloud.	**Teaching steps** 1. **T** reviews and answers questions about the grammar focus and **2A**. 2. **T** introduces **2B**. 3. **Ss** complete **2B** and check answers. 4. **T** introduces **3**. 5. **Ss** complete all exercises in **3**.

Multilevel Organizer: At-a-glance

Opening activities: whole group and cross-ability groups	
Objective Build community and introduce grammar **Materials** Picture B (on CD-ROM) with accompanying audio (on self-study audio CD) **Activity** Tell a story	**Opening activities** ☐ Minutes

Break-out activities: like-ability groups

Objective
Develop level-appropriate language skills

Low-level	Mid-level	High-level	
Facilitator Teacher **Materials** Student's Book and audio Lesson C	**Facilitator** Group Leader **Materials** Student's Book and audio Lesson C	**Facilitator** Independent **Materials** Student's Book and Workbook Lesson C	**Break-out:** **Time 1** ☐ Minutes
Facilitator Group Leader **Materials** Student's Book and audio Lesson C	**Facilitator** Teacher **Materials** Student's Book and Workbook Lesson C	**Facilitator** Independent **Materials** Student's Book and audio Lesson C	**Break-out:** **Time 2** ☐ Minutes
Facilitator Group Leader **Materials** Workbook Lesson C	**Facilitator** Independent **Materials** Workbook Lesson C	**Facilitator** Teacher **Materials** Student's Book Lesson C	**Break-out:** **Time 3** ☐ Minutes

Closing activities: whole group and cross-ability groups	
Objective Assess learning from break-out groups **Materials** Student's Books from each level **Activity** Review grammar	**Closing activities** ☐ Minutes

Multilevel Organizer: Teaching steps

Low-level: Book _____	Mid-level: Book _____	High-level: Book _____

Opening activities: whole group and cross-ability groups

Objective Build community and preview grammar

Facilitator Teacher

Materials Picture B (on CD-ROM) with accompanying audio (Lesson A, **2A** on self-study audio CD)

Activity Tell a story

Teaching steps

1. **T** creates cross-ability groups.
2. **T** shows Picture B and asks **Ss** to agree on answers:
   - Who are the people?
   - Where are they?
   - What are they doing? **OR** What are they talking about?
3. **Ss** share answers and **T** writes answers on board.
4. **T** does one or more of the following:
   - **T** plays audio for Picture B. **Ss** listen and compare with their answers on the board.
   - **Ss** share what they heard and **T** writes responses on board. Low-level **Ss** list vocabulary, higher-level **Ss** retell or write the story.
   - **T** shows a different unit-opening picture from low-level Student's Book and plays accompanying audio. Low-level **Ss** tell the story. Higher-level **Ss** peer-correct.

Break-out activities: like-ability groups (see next page)

Closing activities: whole group and cross-ability groups

Objective Assess learning from break-out groups

Facilitator Teacher

Materials Student's Books from each level

Activity Review grammar

Teaching steps

T does one or more of following:
- On the board, **Ss** write sentences about the pictures. **T** facilitates error correction.
- **Ss** work in cross-ability groups (one **S** from each level), point to Lesson C pictures in their book, and make sentences or ask questions using key structures.
- **Ss** work in cross-ability groups to share information or role-play **3 Communicate**.

Abbreviations used in the organizers

T = teacher   GL = group leader: instructional aide, volunteer, student leader
S = student   Ss = students
Picture A = unit-opening picture from Student's Books Basic, 1, or 2
Picture B = unit-opening picture from Student's Books 3 or 4
1A/2B (any boldfaced numbers and letters) = reference to exercises in the Student's Books

© Cambridge University Press 2009 **Photocopiable**

Break-out activities: like-ability groups

Objective Develop level-appropriate language skills

Break-out: Time 1

Low-level	Mid-level	High-level
Facilitator `Teacher` **Materials** Low-level Student's Book and audio **Teaching steps** 1. **T** introduces **1 Grammar focus**. 2. **T** elicits answers for first two items in **2A**. 3. **Ss** complete exercise and **T** checks answers. If time, **Ss** write answers on board. **T** corrects answers. Optional: **T** plays audio. **Ss** check answers and practice with a partner.	**Facilitator** Group Leader **Materials** Mid-level Student's Book and audio **Teaching steps** 1. **Ss** study **1 Grammar focus**. 2. **Ss** complete **2A**. 3. **GL** or **Ss** check answers using class audio or Teacher's Edition answer key. 4. **Ss** read answers in pairs or small groups.	**Facilitator** Independent **Materials** High-level Student's Book and Workbook **Teaching steps** 1. **T** introduces Workbook Lesson C, points out answer key in Workbook, and leaves group to work independently. 2. **Ss** study **1 Grammar focus** in **Ss** book. 3. **Ss** work in pairs or small groups to complete Lesson C in the Workbook. 4. **Ss** check answers (with Workbook answer key, or with partner and then with answer key).

Break-out: Time 2

Low-level	Mid-level	High-level
Facilitator Group Leader **Materials** Low-level Student's Book **Teaching steps** 1. **GL** reads directions for **2B**. 2. **Ss** complete the exercise. **GL** checks answers using Teacher's Edition answer key. 3. **Ss** continue until all exercises in **2** are completed. 4. **GL** introduces **3**. **Ss** complete all exercises in **3**.	**Facilitator** `Teacher` **Materials** Mid-level Student's Book and Workbook **Teaching steps** 1. **T** reviews **2A** and answers questions. 2. **T** introduces **2B**. 3. **Ss** complete **2B** and **T** checks answers. 4. **T** models **3**. 5. **Ss** complete all exercises in **3**. 6. **T** introduces Workbook Lesson C and points out answer key in Workbook.	**Facilitator** Independent **Materials** High-level Student's Book with audio **Teaching steps** 1. **Ss** review **1 Grammar focus**. 2. **Ss** complete **2A**. 3. **Ss** check answers and practice with a partner. Optional: **Ss** play audio and check answers.

Break-out: Time 3

Low-level	Mid-level	High-level
Facilitator Group Leader	**Facilitator** Independent	**Facilitator** Teacher
Materials Low-level Workbook	**Materials** Mid-level Workbook	**Materials** High-level Student's Book
Teaching steps 1. **GL** introduces Lesson C. 2. **Ss** work in pairs or small groups to complete Lesson C exercises. 3. **GL** checks answers using answer key in Workbook. 4. **Ss** read answers aloud.	**Teaching steps** 1. **Ss** work in pairs or small groups to complete Lesson C exercises. 2. **Ss** check answers using answer key in Workbook. 3. **Ss** practice reading answers aloud.	**Teaching steps** 1. **T** reviews and answers questions about the grammar focus and **2A**. 2. **T** introduces **2B**. 3. **Ss** complete **2B** and check answers. 4. **T** introduces **3**. 5. **Ss** complete all exercises in **3**.

Multilevel Organizer: At-a-glance

Opening activities: whole group	
Objective Build community and focus on reading **Materials** Picture B (on CD-ROM) **Activity** Language Experience – Telling a story	**Opening activities** [ ] Minutes

Break-out activities: like-ability groups

Objective
Develop level-appropriate language skills

Low-level	Mid-level	High-level	
Facilitator Teacher **Materials** Student's Book Lesson D	**Facilitator** Group Leader **Materials** Student's Book and audio Lesson D	**Facilitator** Independent **Materials** Workbook Lesson D	**Break-out:** **Time 1** [ ] Minutes
Facilitator Group Leader **Materials** Student's Book and audio Lesson D	**Facilitator** Teacher **Materials** Student's Book and Workbook Lesson D	**Facilitator** Independent **Materials** Student's Book Lesson D	**Break-out:** **Time 2** [ ] Minutes
Facilitator Group Leader **Materials** Workbook Lesson D	**Facilitator** Independent **Materials** Workbook Lesson D	**Facilitator** Teacher **Materials** Student's Book Lesson D	**Break-out:** **Time 3** [ ] Minutes

Closing activities: whole group and cross-ability groups	
Objective Assess learning from break-out groups **Materials** Student's Books from each level **Activity** Sharing stories	**Closing activities** [ ] Minutes

Multilevel Organizer: Teaching steps

Low-level: Book _____	Mid-level: Book _____	High-level: Book _____

Opening activities: whole group

Objective Build community and focus on reading

Facilitator Teacher

Materials Picture B (on CD-ROM)

Activity Language Experience – Telling a story

Teaching steps

1. **T** elicits words and sentences about the pictures and writes them on the board. **Ss** repeat words / sentences.
2. **T** asks **Ss** to use words / sentences to tell a story about the pictures.
3. **T** writes story on the board. **Ss** read and revise the story.
4. **T** does one or more of the following:
   - **Ss** read the story aloud (low-level **Ss**).
   - **Ss** retell the story using their own words (mid-level **Ss**).
   - **Ss** predict a new ending for the story (high-level **Ss**).

Break-out activities: like-ability groups (see next page)

Closing activities: whole group and cross-ability groups

Objective Assess learning from break-out groups

Facilitator Teacher

Materials Student's Books from each level

Activity Sharing stories

Teaching steps

T does one or more of the following:

- **T** poses general questions about the reading that work across levels (e.g., *Who is the reading about? What did you learn about the person?*). **T** puts **Ss** in cross-ability groups (one **S** from each break-out group), and **Ss** share information about their story within their group.
- **Ss** in cross-ability groups (one **S** from each group) read their Lesson D stories aloud and teach new vocabulary.
- **T** invites **S** from each group to read his / her Lesson D story to the class. Class asks questions (low-level **Ss** ask about vocabulary; mid-level **Ss** ask about confusing sentences; high-level **Ss** ask about details).
- **T** invites **Ss** from low- or mid-level groups to teach vocabulary in **4 Picture Dictionary**.

Abbreviations used in the organizers

T = teacher   GL = group leader: instructional aide, volunteer, student leader
S = student   Ss = students
Picture A = unit-opening picture from Student's Books Basic, 1, or 2
Picture B = unit-opening picture from Student's Books 3 or 4
1A/2B (any boldfaced numbers and letters) = reference to exercises in the Student's Books

Break-out activities: like-ability groups

Objective Develop level-appropriate language skills

Break-out: Time 1

Low-level	Mid-level	High-level
Facilitator Teacher **Materials** Low-level Student's Book **Teaching steps** 1. T leads discussion in **1**. 2. T reads story in **2**. 3. T points out reading tip and elicits examples in the reading (Books 1–4 only). 4. T introduces **3**. 5. Ss complete **3** and share answers. T corrects. 6. T introduces **4**.	**Facilitator** Group Leader **Materials** Mid-level Student's Book and audio **Teaching steps** 1. In pairs, Ss complete **1**. 2. Ss play audio for **2** and read. 3. Ss complete exercise **3** (Books 1 and 2) or **3A** (Books 3 and 4).	**Facilitator** Independent **Materials** High-level Workbook **Teaching steps** 1. T introduces Workbook Lesson D, points out answer key in Workbook, and leaves group to work independently. 2. Ss work in pairs or small groups to complete exercises. 3. Ss check answers (with answer key, or with partner and then with answer key).

Break-out: Time 2

Low-level	Mid-level	High-level
Facilitator Group Leader **Materials** Low-level Student's Book and audio **Teaching steps** 1. Ss complete **4A**. 2. GL plays audio and Ss check answers. 3. GL checks answers using audio script or Teacher's Edition answer key. 4. GL introduces **4B**. 5. Ss work in pairs and practice conversation.	**Facilitator** Teacher **Materials** Mid-level Student's Book and Workbook **Teaching steps** 1. T checks exercises and answers questions. 2. T points out reading tip and elicits examples in the reading. 3. T introduces **4** (Books 1 and 2) or **3B** and **3C** (Books 3 and 4). 4. Ss complete exercises and T corrects. 5. T introduces Workbook Lesson D and points out answer key in Workbook.	**Facilitator** Independent **Materials** High-Level Student's Book **Teaching steps** 1. In pairs, Ss complete **1**. 2. Ss read the story. 3. Ss complete **3** (Books 1 and 2) or **3A** (Books 3 and 4).

Break-out: Time 3

Low-level	Mid-level	High-level
Facilitator Group Leader	**Facilitator** Independent	**Facilitator** Teacher
Materials Low-level Workbook	**Materials** Mid-level Workbook	**Materials** High-level Student's Book
Teaching steps 1. **GL** introduces Lesson D. 2. **Ss** work in pairs or small groups to complete Lesson D exercises. 3. **GL** checks answers using answer key in Workbook. 4. **Ss** read answers aloud.	**Teaching steps** 1. **Ss** work in pairs or small groups to complete Lesson D exercises. 2. **Ss** check answers using answer key in Workbook. 3. **Ss** practice reading answers aloud.	**Teaching steps** 1. **T** corrects exercises. 2. **T** points out reading tip and elicits examples in the reading. Optional: **T** may play audio for **Ss** to listen as they read to themselves. 3. **T** models pronunciation of key vocabulary from **4 Picture dictionary** (Books 1 and 2) or **3B Build your vocabulary** (Books 3 and 4). 4. **Ss** complete exercises and **T** corrects.

Multilevel Organizer: At-a-glance

Opening activities: whole group and cross-ability groups	Opening activities
Objective Build community and focus on writing **Materials** Picture A (on CD-ROM) **Activity** Writing at the word / phrase / sentence level	☐ Minutes

Break-out activities: like-ability groups

Objective
Develop level-appropriate language skills

Low-level	Mid-level	High-level	
Facilitator `Teacher` **Materials** Student's Book Lesson E	**Facilitator** Group Leader **Materials** Student's Book Lesson E	**Facilitator** Independent **Materials** Workbook Lesson E	**Break-out:** **Time 1** ☐ Minutes
Facilitator Group Leader **Materials** Student's Book Lesson E	**Facilitator** `Teacher` **Materials** Student's Book and Workbook Lesson E	**Facilitator** Independent **Materials** Student's Book Lesson E	**Break-out:** **Time 2** ☐ Minutes
Facilitator Group Leader **Materials** Workbook Lesson E	**Facilitator** Independent **Materials** Workbook Lesson E	**Facilitator** `Teacher` **Materials** Student's Book Lesson E	**Break-out:** **Time 3** ☐ Minutes

Closing activities: whole group	Closing activities
Objective Assess learning from break-out groups **Materials** Student writing samples from each level **Activity** Gallery walk	☐ Minutes

Multilevel Organizer: Teaching steps

Low-level: Book _____	Mid-level: Book _____	High-level: Book _____

Opening activities: whole group and cross-ability groups

Objective Build community and focus on writing

Facilitator Teacher

Materials Picture A (on CD-ROM)

Activity Writing at the word / phrase / sentence level

Teaching steps

1. **T** elicits vocabulary from Picture A.
2. **Ss** write words (lower-level **Ss**) and sentences (higher-level **Ss**) on board.
3. **T** facilitates error correction of words / sentences.
4. **T** does one or more of the following:
   - **T** or **S** dictates words / sentences. Other **Ss** write.
   - **Ss** in cross-ability groups use words / sentences to write a story. **Ss** share with class.
   - **T** points to items / actions in Picture A. **Ss** write words / sentences.

Break-out activities: like-ability groups (see next page)

Closing activities: whole group

Objective Assess learning from break-out groups

Facilitator Teacher

Materials Ss' writings from Lesson E

Activity Gallery walk

Teaching steps

1. **T** posts **Ss'** writings around room.
2. **T** invites **Ss** to circulate and read the writings.
3. **Ss** answer one or more of the following questions:
   - What did you like?
   - What did you learn?
   - What do you want to ask?

Abbreviations used in the organizers

T = teacher   GL = group leader: instructional aide, volunteer, student leader
S = student   Ss = students
Picture A = unit-opening picture from Student's Books Basic, 1, or 2
Picture B = unit-opening picture from Student's Books 3 or 4
1A/2B (any boldfaced numbers and letters) = reference to exercises in the Student's Books

Break-out activities: like-ability groups

Objective Develop level-appropriate language skills

Break-out: Time 1

Low-level	Mid-level	High-level
Facilitator Teacher **Materials** Low-level Student's Book **Teaching steps** 1. **T** introduces **1** and helps **Ss** complete the exercises. 2. **T** corrects exercises in **1**. 3. **T** points out the writing model. 4. **T** introduces writing tip and elicits examples in the writing model (Books 1–4 only). 5. **T** introduces **2**.	**Facilitator** Group Leader **Materials** Mid-level Student's Book **Teaching steps** 1. **GL** or **Ss** read the directions in **1**. 2. **Ss** work in pairs or small groups to complete the exercises in **1** and share answers. 3. **Ss** study the writing model and list questions for **T**.	**Facilitator** Independent **Materials** High-level Workbook **Teaching steps** 1. **T** introduces Workbook Lesson E, points out answer key in Workbook, and leaves group to work independently. 2. **Ss** work in pairs or small groups to complete Lesson E exercises. 3. **Ss** check answers (with Workbook answer key, or with partner and then with answer key).

Break-out: Time 2

Low-level	Mid-level	High-level
Facilitator Group Leader **Materials** Low-level Student's Book **Teaching steps** 1. **GL** reviews **2** task and writing model in **1**. 2. **Ss** write on separate sheet of paper. 3. **GL** assists **Ss** in completing **3**. 4. **GL** collects papers for **T**.	**Facilitator** Teacher **Materials** Mid-level Student's Book and Workbook **Teaching steps** 1. **T** corrects exercises in **1** and answers questions. 2. **T** points out writing tip. 3. **T** introduces **2**. 4. **Ss** write on separate sheet of paper. 5. **T** assists **Ss** in completing **3**. 6. **T** introduces Workbook Lesson E and points out answer key in Workbook.	**Facilitator** Independent **Materials** High-level Student's Book **Teaching steps** 1. **Ss** read the direction lines and complete the exercises in **1**. 2. **Ss** share answers and list questions for **T**. 3. **Ss** study the writing model.

Break-out: Time 3

Low-level	Mid-level	High-level
Facilitator Group Leader	**Facilitator** Independent	**Facilitator** Teacher
Materials Low-level Workbook	**Materials** Mid-level Workbook	**Materials** High-level Student's Book
Teaching steps 1. **GL** introduces Lesson E. 2. **Ss** work in pairs or small groups to complete Lesson E exercises. 3. **Ss** compare answers and share writing. 4. **GL** checks answers using answer key in Workbook.	**Teaching steps** 1. **Ss** work in pairs or small groups to complete Lesson E exercises. 2. **Ss** compare answers. 3. **Ss** check answers using answer key in Workbook. 4. **Ss** practice reading answers aloud.	**Teaching steps** 1. **T** corrects exercises in **1** and answers questions. 2. **T** points out writing tip and elicits examples from writing model. 3. **T** introduces **2**. 4. **Ss** write on separate sheet of paper. 5. **T** assists **Ss** in completing **3**.

Multilevel Organizer: At-a-glance

Opening activities: whole group

Objective
Build community and focus on life-skills reading

Materials
Life-skills reading from low-level Student's Book

Activity
Scan for information

Opening activities

[ ] Minutes

Break-out activities: like-ability groups

Objective
Develop level-appropriate language skills

Low-level	Mid-level	High-level	
Facilitator Teacher **Materials** Student's Book Lesson F	**Facilitator** Group Leader **Materials** Student's Book Lesson F	**Facilitator** Independent **Materials** Workbook Lesson F	**Break-out: Time 1** [ ] Minutes
Facilitator Group Leader **Materials** Student's Book Lesson F	**Facilitator** Teacher **Materials** Student's Book and Workbook Lesson F	**Facilitator** Independent **Materials** Student's Book Lesson F	**Break-out: Time 2** [ ] Minutes
Facilitator Group Leader **Materials** Workbook Lesson F	**Facilitator** Independent **Materials** Workbook Lesson F	**Facilitator** Teacher **Materials** Student's Book Lesson F	**Break-out: Time 3** [ ] Minutes

Closing activities: whole group and cross-ability groups

Objective
Assess learning from break-out groups

Materials
Lesson F, Fun with Language; Self-assessments

Activity
Language games

Closing activities

[ ] Minutes

Multilevel Organizer: Teaching steps

Low-level: Book _____	Mid-level: Book _____	High-level: Book _____

Opening activities: whole group

Objective Build community and focus on life-skills reading

Facilitator Teacher

Materials Life-skills reading from low-level Student's Book

Activity Scanning

Teaching steps

1. **T** asks questions to focus on schema and develop scanning skills.
   - What is the heading?
   - What is the format? (table, chart, graph)
   - What are the key parts? (name, number, location, personal information)
2. If time allows, **T** selects a different life-skills reading from Lesson F in another level of the Student's Books and repeats process.

Note: In whole-group activities, it is recommended to select life-skills readings from lower-level groups. This provides lower-level **Ss** with additional practice and builds self-confidence. It also naturally encourages cross-ability tutoring by higher-level **Ss**.

Break-out activities: like-ability groups (see next page)

Closing activities: whole group and cross-ability groups

Objective Assess learning from break-out groups

Facilitator Teacher

Materials Lesson F, Fun with language; wrap-up exercise

Activity Language game; Self-assessment

Teaching steps

T does one or more of the following:
- **T** selects one Lesson F exercise and teaches it to the whole class.
- In cross-ability groups, low-level **Ss** teach higher-level **Ss** a Lesson F exercise from low-level Student's Book.
- **Ss** from each level volunteer to teach Lesson F exercise to whole group.
- **Ss** complete unit self-assessment in their Student's Book. In like-ability or cross-ability groups, **Ss** help each other with problem topics.

Abbreviations used in the organizers

T = teacher   GL = group leader: instructional aide, volunteer, student leader

S = student   Ss = students

Picture A = unit-opening picture from Student's Books Basic, 1, or 2

Picture B = unit-opening picture from Student's Books 3 or 4

1A/2B (any boldfaced numbers and letters) = reference to exercises in the Student's Books

Break-out activities: like-ability groups

Objective Develop level-appropriate language skills

Break-out: Time 1

Low-level	Mid-level	High-level
Facilitator Teacher **Materials** Low-level Student's Book **Teaching steps** 1. **T** introduces **1**. 2. **T** reads questions in **1A** and students locate answers. **T** corrects answers. 3. **T** reads direction line for **1B**. **Ss** complete the exercise. 4. **T** introduces **2A**.	**Facilitator** Group Leader **Materials** Mid-level Student's Book **Teaching steps** 1. **Ss** read **1 Life-skills reading**. 2. **Ss** answer questions in **1A**. 3. **GL** or **Ss** check answers in Teacher's Edition answer key. 4. **Ss** work in pairs and complete **1B**.	**Facilitator** Independent **Materials** High-level Workbook **Teaching steps** 1. **T** introduces Workbook Lesson F, points out answer key, and leaves group to work independently. 2. **Ss** work in pairs or small groups to complete Lesson F exercises. 3. **Ss** check answers (with Workbook answer key, or with partner and then with answer key).

Break-out: Time 2

Low-level	Mid-level	High-level
Facilitator Group Leader **Materials** Low-level Student's Book **Teaching steps** 1. **GL** reviews **2A** instructions. **Ss** complete exercise **2A**. 2. **GL** checks answers. Optional: **GL** checks answers in Teacher's Edition answer key. 3. **Ss** complete remaining exercises and share answers.	**Facilitator** Teacher **Materials** Mid-level Student's Book and Workbook **Teaching steps** 1. **T** reviews exercises in **1** and identifies the type of life-skills reading. 2. **T** introduces **2A**. 3. **Ss** complete exercise and share answers. 4. **T** introduces **2B** and **Ss** do activity. 5. **T** introduces Workbook Lesson F and points out answer key in Workbook.	**Facilitator** Independent **Materials** High-level Student's Book **Teaching steps** 1. **Ss** read **1 Life-skills reading**. 2. **Ss** answer questions in **1A**. 3. **Ss** compares answers. 4. **Ss** work in pairs and complete **1B**.

Break-out: Time 3

Low-level	Mid-level	High-level
Facilitator Group Leader	**Facilitator** Independent	**Facilitator** **Teacher**
Materials Low-level Workbook	**Materials** Mid-level Workbook	**Materials** High-level Student's Book
Teaching steps 1. **GL** introduces Lesson F. 2. **Ss** work in pairs or small groups to complete Lesson F exercises. 3. **GL** checks answers using answer key. 4. **Ss** read answers aloud.	**Teaching steps** 1. **Ss** work in pairs or small groups to complete Lesson F exercises. 2. **Ss** compare answers. 3. **Ss** check answers using answer key in Workbook. 4. **Ss** practice reading answers.	**Teaching steps** 1. **T** reviews exercises in **1** and identifies the type of life-skills reading. 2. **T** introduces **2A**. 3. **Ss** complete **2A** and share answers. 4. **T** introduces **2B** and **Ss** do activity.

Ventures **Multilevel Organizer: Teaching steps**

Multilevel Lesson Plan Template: At-a-glance

Unit _____ **Lesson** _____

Opening activities: whole group	
Objective **Materials** **Activity**	**Opening activities** ☐ Minutes

Break-out activities: like-ability groups **Objective**			
Low-level	**Mid-level**	**High-level**	
Facilitator **Materials**	**Facilitator** **Materials**	**Facilitator** **Materials**	**Break-out:** **Time 1** ☐ Minutes
Facilitator **Materials**	**Facilitator** **Materials**	**Facilitator** **Materials**	**Break-out:** **Time 2** ☐ Minutes
Facilitator **Materials**	**Facilitator** **Materials**	**Facilitator** **Materials**	**Break-out:** **Time 3** ☐ Minutes

Closing activities: whole group and cross-ability groups	
Objective **Materials** **Activity**	**Closing activities** ☐ Minutes

Multilevel Lesson Plan Template: Teaching steps

Unit _____ Lesson _____

Low-level: Book _____	Mid-level: Book _____	High-level: Book _____

Opening activities: whole group

Objective

Facilitator

Materials

Activity

Teaching steps

Break-out activities: like-ability groups (see next page)

Closing activities: whole group and cross-ability groups

Objective

Facilitator

Materials

Activity

Teaching steps

Unit _____ Lesson _____

Break-out activities: like-ability groups
Objective:

Break-out: Time 1

Low-level	Mid-level	High-level
Facilitator Materials Teaching steps	Facilitator Materials Teaching steps	Facilitator Materials Teaching steps

Break-out: Time 2

Low-level	Mid-level	High-level
Facilitator Materials Teaching steps	Facilitator Materials Teaching steps	Facilitator Materials Teaching steps

Unit _____ Lesson _____

Break-out: Time 3

Low-level	Mid-level	High-level
Facilitator Materials Teaching steps	Facilitator Materials Teaching steps	Facilitator Materials Teaching steps

Ventures Multilevel Lesson Plan Template: Teaching steps